THE CRIES OF A DIVORCED PASTOR

GOD WILL TALK YOU THROUGH IT

VICTOR L. POWELL

Bridgeport, CT 06605
www.hovpub.com

The Cries of a Divorced Pastor

GOD WILL TALK YOU THROUGH IT

HOV Publishing a division of HOV, LLC.
www.hovpub.com
hopeofvision@gmail.com

Front Cover Design by Ke'Cia Griffin and Morenda Wysinger
Inside layout by Hope of Vision Designs
Editor/Proofread: HOV Publishing Editorial Team

Contact the Author, Victor L Powell at vlpthinkbig@icloud.com

For further information regarding special discounts on bulk purchases, please visit www.hovpub.com

ISBN Paperback: 978-1-955107-80-8
ISBN eBook: 978-1-955107-79-2

Printed in the United States of America

Dedication

"This Book is dedicated to anyone who has lived and cried their way through shame, guilt and disappointment and is OVERCOMING..."

Special Thanks

To all my special contributors who keep encouraging me to write and empower people to live and press through the pains of life.

Introduction

My first book was entitled, *Closet Ministry* which dealt with various principles of prayer. Written almost twenty years ago, I dealt with what I believed was the missing piece in the universal church at that time: the ministry of prayer. The concept behind prayer being a missing ministry was the advent of other areas of focus in the Body of Christ. So many churches were catering to ministry areas such as children, media, stewardship, and other areas, but one of the less emphasized areas of ministry was the ministry of prayer. The aim of *Closet Ministry* was to stimulate and provide insight for the church to reprioritize getting back into the "closet" of prayer as referenced in the book of Matthew, chapter 6. Jesus instructed the church to "enter the closet" to pray and spend time alone with God. I still believe that is definitely a concept that is very useful and we, as believers, need to embrace it as a personal part of our lives. In addition, I now believe that because we went through an era of rebuking demonic forces and warfare and talking more to those demonic forces than to God, those concepts are very real and biblical; however, as I began to examine the ministry of Jesus and realized that when Jesus was bringing a person through a situation, it was not actually through prayer. It was more through a conversation.

From 2012 until now, I have gone through a critical season in my life. I found myself having more conversations with God and the Holy Spirit responding to me conversationally. A great example of this is found in John chapter 4 when Jesus met the Samaritan woman at the well. Jesus had a conversation with her. She did not pray. She talked with Him, and Jesus talked with her. Jesus talked her through the multiplicities of her relationships by meeting her through conversation. I was like, "Wow! We've missed this!" It was an intimate conversational relationship with our God. We find throughout Scripture that when Jesus met with Peter, James, and John, in particular, He had a conversation with them. On several occasions, Jesus conversationally articulated his thoughts, so I started seeing all these conversations, i.e. personal engagements, between Jesus and others. Another such example is the conversation Jesus had with Nicodemus about what it truly meant to be born again (John 3). All these life-changing encounters were not through prayer as we have believed it to be, but through conversations with Divinity.

I have struggled through seasons of warfare and crisis because I could not simply bind and loose, shake, holler and scream. All I could do was talk to the Father and allow Him to talk to me. Every subject He talked to me about was profound because I had all these conversations going on in my mind about my imperfections, condemnation, whether I could have a ministry after a divorce, guilt, shame, forgiveness; wondering about all the people that walked away because I did not articulate or explain to them my struggles, trials, secret hurts, pain. I wondered whether I would ever be happy or have joy. I struggled with whether or not people would ever see my value despite my mistakes or faults. I wondered if people would see the beauty of marriage and my divorce is not a way of my saying I do not like marriage. The pain of all these inner voices opened the door for the Holy Spirit to talk with me and talk me through my inner insecurities. This book is about a conversation with God and He will talk you through it. I want to introduce to you perhaps another style of prayer. The Holy Spirit truly wants to talk to us and talk us through our pain, our shame, and any disappointments.

Contents

Chapter 1

Living the Lie
A Culture of Adultery

Mayors, Governors, Senators, cabinet members, Presidents, and yes, Pastors and church leaders are all guilty. Of what? Why cheating, of course. It happens from the mayor's office to the state senate to the halls of the Senate to the White House. Not only that, this year alone, nearly half of all married couples – 2.7 of every 6.1 – will divorce. That amounts to about a divorce every 13 seconds.

More than 2.4 million divorces in 2021 alone. Chew on all that for a moment.

Not only that, this year alone, nearly half of all married couples – 2.7 of every 6.1 – will divorce.

The numbers are staggering.

I'll bet you never stopped to think about this. Most people, whether they attend church or not, don't mind if you live a lie. They would prefer married couples stay together no matter what. In fact, if you're a leader of any sort, people want you to remain together even when the relationship is clearly dysfunctional or not functioning. They would rather tolerate or pretend not to see you in an adulterous relationship than to have you end a marriage that no longer works. Live the lie even though both people are depressed and miserable.

You see, adultery is accepted while divorce is rejected. This account is my story about coming to a very personal decision about my life and marriage. It is in no case a story intended to disparage my ex-wife. It is instead my discovery, my journey into happiness. It is an account of my pain, my rejection of my internal happiness, not the external slaughter and criticism of anyone, particularly my ex-wife.

During my tenure as a spiritual leader, having been called to ministry in 1981 and to a senior pastor role in 1990, I have observed many things as you can imagine. Specifically, I am aware of leaders who had affairs, who had children outside their marriages, who led clandestine homosexual lifestyles, who (by their own accounts) were miserable in their marriages, and some who divorced. All these things require repentance and forgiveness. Even so, these men were not subject to the dismantling of their leadership roles neither were they rejected by the Christian community when what they were doing was uncovered. I also found that the whole pastor and first lady image is preferred to living in truth. It is that image that in so many instances has led to the establishment of a culture of adultery. People would rather continue seeing the image of their spiritual leader and his wife together in a pseudo happy relationship than see them go through a divorce and possibly find some measure of peace and happiness apart from each other.

The Culture of Selective Grace

Some sins, failures, and falls are selected for strong grace. While it may not necessarily be specific to every pastor or church, denomination or organization, or religious group, I have both observed and experienced, within the secret culture of the church, that a person can be adulterous, homosexual, depressed, disappointed, and oppressed, but as long as s/he maintains the image people hold of spiritual leadership, in particular, the image of the perfect "first family," church folks will tolerate their bad behavior. Interestingly, those leaders find grace even when everyone knows that privately their religious leaders are leading double lives. People excuse their bad behavior with statements such as, "A man will be a man" or "All have sinned" or "Everybody has a little sin." They are cultural, social acceptances that are given grace unconditionally.

However, once that flawless image of the picture-perfect first family has been crushed and sliced, grace is not administered quite so liberally. Restoration is not handed out as generously. Consider this: a couple learned of the difficulties their pastor was having in his relationship that subsequently led to a divorce. They left the ministry because they objected to the pastor's decision to end his marriage and connected to another ministry. Later that couple went through a divorce themselves.

Thus, my observation of this mentality is that we are selective in how we issue grace because it affects our own images and perceptions of the perfection of leaders. The thinking behind this selective grace is that these leaders are models and images of perfection, not fallible leaders and human beings. Certainly, leaders should be models for their extended communities, congregations, and families; beyond that, they should strive to be excellent in spirit – men and women of integrity. That should be the goal of leaders. At the same time, they should be working through their humanity without feeling that if they experience some level of failure, the same level of grace won't be extended to them in case they need it.

It's like an insurance policy. If you are an insurance salesman, you constantly give away/sell the policy of redemption, sell the policy of grace, sell the policy of God's unconditional love without having an insurance policy for yourself. There are, unfortunately, situations where leaders need the same insurance policy, but instead, they have theirs ruled invalid. The same heavenly Father that they helped thousands discover His love, His mercy, His grace, His redemption, His correction, His instruction, will not extend to you, the leader, the same grace you have given away, or so you are made to believe. That same grace that you have given away somehow does not extend to you.

These were the conversations I had with God and the cries of my heart. I found that many people cut me off, threw me away, and threw my ministry away because of a trying experience. There were few exceptions to that among the many people to whom I was connected; only a few men of God reached out to me. It was an experience that was heart-wrenching and unforgettable when I was going through it, particularly having few people extend grace to me. From a biblical perspective, there is only one unforgiveable sin – to blaspheme the Holy Spirit. A person choosing to divorce, whether by personal decision or the decision of a spouse, still falls in the parameters of God's redemptive love, forgiveness, mercy, and grace. Remember though, all of us as believers of scripture should do all we can to work through considerations of divorce and to keep our marriages intact, if possible.

Further, if divorce becomes the choice, shouldn't the church embrace the divorcee with the same love, kindness, and mercy that God extends to adulterers, fornicators, or women who have children out of wedlock. (Strange how it is the female who has a baby out of wedlock, not the male who releases the sperm. He's not a fornicator; the girl is.) While there may be a sin problem in the universal church, there is certainly an image and a selective grace problem, also. It's almost as if people will give you grace until you get caught and you negatively affect the image the church has of you. A woman having a baby out of wedlock affects the image of the church. She's judged because her pregnancy shows while the man is allowed to move on without blame. A man or woman of God going through a divorce affects the image of the church. If a leader goes through a divorce or some other public situation, that also affects the image of the church. Note that when the secret culture remains a secret, the church remains intact. So, what can we conclude? Well, I didn't see that grace was unconditional in many cases. The cry of the heart of many stemmed from the alienation and distance they felt because of private decisions they made that had public ramifications. The question is, what should be the church's biblical response to a leader who may unfortunately go through something that affects the image of the church? First, there should always be distance and the extension of grace for the leader to have a problem. Give the leader distance, space, room to have a problem. Secondly, there should always be the same extension of grace given to the leader that s/he extended to others and that Heavenly Father has given all of us – the same grace. Next, consider if the leader is biblically broken or repentant over his/her decision, no matter who was at fault for the relationship's failure? Fourth, the church should seek methods for redemptive restoration to salvage the leader's ministry, particularly if s/he is broken and contrite, according to God's standards, about their decisions. No matter whether the issue is adultery or divorce, his fault, her fault, both their fault, is God's grace conditional toward that in those situations or not? I see from a biblical perspective that God's grace is not selective. Instead, His grace is extensive. It is indescribable. It is immeasurable. That's how I see God's grace. For that leader who is reading this and may be self-condemning or self-doubting, cry no more! To the one who may be down on himself or who had many people walk away from him/her, look up! For the one who has been ostracized and cut off, I have come to tell you that God's grace is, indeed, unconditional. It is also corrective, instructional, and new. His grace can give you a new and fresh opportunity, a new audience that knows nothing of your so-called failure. His grace is restorative and can relocate you physically, emotionally, and spiritually, giving you new opportunities in a new season of your life. His grace extends to us the wonderful privilege of learning from past mistakes. To the leader who found himself crying over pain, failures, or faults, I am not excusing anyone's failings, falls, or mistakes. What I am saying is that His grace is sufficient. You can begin anew and experience the unconditional love and grace of the living God. Pray with me now for that love. No matter what the culture of your church, organization, or denomination, your city or community, His loving grace can give you a new opportunity.

> Prayer: *Father, we thank You that Your grace is not selective or biased. There's nothing Your grace cannot forgive, restore, renew, or redeem. I thank You that I, through Your grace, am able to release myself from guilt, shame, pride, ego, darkness, and even my bad decisions about divorce, adultery, or fornication. I thank You that I am forgiven and restored...redeemed by the grace of God. In Jesus' name.* Amen.

Chapter 2

Unreligious Conversation

As I get older, I am moved by the reality that Jesus talked so many people through their healing and process, and in my journey with God, I have found that we are having more conversations now rather than what we have come to know as the traditional concept of prayer. Just look at Jesus' encounter with the woman at the well. She was in a crisis of relationship, married numerous times, so obviously there is an emptiness inside her. She attempted to fill that emptiness with her husbands and found herself at the end of herself when she encountered Jesus. Traditionally, when you look at that situation from a contemporary perspective, her dilemma should have required fasting and hours of prayer as we know it.

We can assume she tried intense fasting and prayer, but none of those things turned her deep longing around. It is no longer uncommon in our present culture to know people who have been married several times, and if not married, they have had numerous relationships. It is also not uncommon to meet people with deep voids that they attempt to fill through drugs, alcohol, and illicit sex. When we look at the woman at the well, we see a covenant-minded woman who made several bad relationship decisions. Isn't it interesting that one conversation with Jesus (God) turned her life around? She had one dialogue with Christ, and He turned a lifetime of bad decisions around. He talked her through her horrible history of bad decisions and relationships IN ONE ENCOUNTER.

I think the concept of prayer we practice is more religious than it is conversational. A relationship is inclusive of intimacy. Intimacy is inclusive of conversation. A relationship involves a two-way conversation. Jesus asked the woman a few questions, and she answered truthfully and honestly. She left their encounter transformed through the dialogue. He did not entangle her with religion or the Law but established a relationship with her that was born out of a conversation. Again, in one conversation, he talked her through a lifetime of unwholesome decisions. I am amazed that I never saw this reality before. After many years of being a student of God's Word, I never saw that many principles that God revealed through Christ were more conversational than they were religious.

There are several principles we should learn from this revelation:

1. **Abandon the religious concept of communicating with God.** You do not have to be in a certain position (posture) to talk to God. You do not have to be on your knees or bowed with your eyes closed. You do not have to say certain things to God to get him to hear you. Your dialogue does not have to be filled with deep terminology and theological language. Abandon that religious view or concept of God!

2. **God wants to relate to you as a Father, and you, His child, as a son or daughter.**

3. **God wants to talk you through your pain, not yell you**

through your pain. God does not want to beat you up through your pain. He wants to talk with you and walk you through, to encourage and strengthen you.

4. **Just as Jesus brought out the best in the woman at the well through conversation, He wants to bring out the best in you through conversation.** The conversation long ago did not have judgment or condemnation. Instead, it led her to the best part of herself. What a powerful concept! The Holy Spirit wants to lead you to a conversation that brings out the best in you! Not judgment. Not criticism. Not self-criticism, but awareness of self that leads to the best part of yourself. He loves you, so you can become phenomenal!

Chapter 3

The Gift of Imperfection

I am amazed at the things God has talked me through in my life. This chapter deals with the "gift" of imperfection. What I came to realize is that God had to talk me through this crazy notion that I had to have it all together. I prided myself on things I had never done before or would not do and spent almost a lifetime feeding the idolatry of having a clean-cut reputation. I prided myself on what I had not done as it related to looking at other people. What bondage I put myself in! Perfection created a paranoia that took freedom away from me. It took happiness away from me because it created the over-consumption of worrying about what people thought of me or would say about me. People's opinions became idolatrous, and I had no freedom or peace of mind because my entire life was wrapped up in appearance: my need to be perfect or to appear perfect to others. This kind of thinking produced arrogance in me and created a prison for me.

You may be asking why I am calling this chapter "The Gift of Imperfection?" As I transitioned through a divorce, I realized that I was not going to avoid the opinions of people nor escape a hit to my reputation. I also realized that it was the end of a euphoric good name, and I was now being handed the gift of imperfection. A limp. A hit. Criticism at another level, and that it was, in fact, a release *into* freedom. I realized that now I did not have to live as if I didn't have a blemish on my life. Now I do not have to live as if I am perfect. Wow! I am really free. I am like other men. Not from the perspective of being a follower or afraid to be different, but now I have a sense of identification. Jesus was "in touch with the feelings of our infirmities" (Hebrews 4), and now I have the freedom of knowing and accepting my infirmities. The illusion that I did not have an infirmity is deception. The illusion that I was not like other men was deception as well, but to come into the revelation of this as a *gift* of imperfection allows me to feel, touch, and identify with those I am attempting to impact for the glory of God. As I look at God's Word, I have now come to understand/ realize that He talks us through all our imperfections and *perfectly* uses our imperfections. Jesus talked to the woman at the well through her imperfections and perfectly used her imperfections as a message to her sphere of influence. God also used the disciple Peter through his imperfections. God used Moses and his imperfections to reach an imperfect creation (creature/being?). Man /Adam was CREATED as a perfect being, with dominion over the things on earth, but he sinned by eating the forbidden fruit in the garden. God perfectly uses imperfections.

He talks us through all our imperfections and *perfectly* uses our imperfections.

For thirty-five years of my life, I preached a message that I did not truly believe: that we are made perfect through weakness (2 Corinthians 12:9), and grace uses our imperfections to preach a perfect message to touch/reach an imperfect world. It's a gift. I don't have to pretend. I don't have to act or fake it. I don't have to pretend that I have never fallen before. It is freedom. It is God's grace at work in me and the power of God working through me. Not my righteousness or perfection nor my illusion of having it all together. It is moving under the power of grace through brokenness. It is God using broken people to touch a broken world. Only a perfect God can do that!

God handed me a gift that I do not know if I had ever experienced before. God had to talk me through this realization to get me to this place. I had so many questions. I wondered what people were going to think. How am I going to be viewed? The illusion that I wasn't viewed before my failure was deception, but it took this critical moment and turning point in my life to experience grace at a level I had never experienced before. God handed me the gift of imperfection; He handed me freedom. I want to hand you these principles to freedom:

1. **There is nowhere in Scripture (What about Old Testament *Job* 1:1?) where God uses perfect people.** He hands each of His vessels the need for grace which is a gift. He does this, so the message we convey is not tainted with self-righteousness or arrogance. The message is touched with the blood

of Jesus Christ; therefore, I can identify with the people I am reaching. Grace is New Testament teaching with the coming of Christ.

2. **God will never truly be able to use us without a deep revelation of His grace.**

3. **God has to heal us and deliver us from the need to hide.**

4. **As long as we have an assumption of my imperfection, we will not have a true revelation of His grace.**

God handed me the gift of imperfection. I am so delighted that I lived long enough to know His grace, love, and forgiveness. Perhaps now, I'm useable.

Chapter 4

God Is Not Difficult

As I looked at all the prototypes of available Christian information, I began to see why many people run away from God as perceived by/through organized religion. I have concluded that we make God look difficult/lofty, condescending, and unapproachable. We make Him look unreachable. We make God look judgmental and critical. The Church has presented God as a non-relational being/entity, and a God of punishment, hurt, and pain. It is hard to see and embrace the love of God when I have to go through too many steps. Through my process of starting over after the pain of a divorce, I had to find a simple God. I had to find a God who would simply be my Father. I started to relate to Matthew 6 at an entirely different level. Jesus instructed us to pray, "Our Father," and that is the God I had to find. I had to find the God who was simply a father, and I was simply His son. As scripture says, "I will be a Father to you and you will be my sons and daughters, says the Lord Almighty" (2 Cor 6:18). What a profound understanding we need to give to the Body of Christ! The Apostle Paul talked about the simplicity of Christ. The simplicity of Christ is merely getting to know Him and Him getting to know me (Christ ALREADY knows; HE is OMNIPOTENT, OMNIPRESENT). Simple intimacy. My journey took me into a dismantling of all of the knowledge of the Old Testament steps of getting to God. I wrote about these steps in my first book, *Closet Ministry*. I believe it was revelation as a tool that has eventually led me to the simplicity of getting to know God— the place I am right now: The Tabernacle of Moses which deals with the outer court, the inner court, and the Most Holy Place.

Ultimately, God's heart was Moses' Tabernacle to be a pattern or steps to the simplicity of who God is. It may have appeared to be difficult at one time, but in Christ, God took away all difficulties on the path to getting to know God. Suddenly, God began to open up about how I saw Him as a father differently. I started just calling upon His name and He simply answered. I also started seeing the simplicity of Christ differently. For example, I could simply ask, knock, and seek. I started seeing the simplicity of a relationship with God in a new and revelatory way. In a time of crisis, I found that I needed to take away the difficulty of overthinking/ overreaching God/worship. I had to move away from binding and loosening the devil or having to go through a cleansing process to get to God. I had to rid myself of the thought that God was so far away; of overcoming an overwhelming consciousness that God was unreachable because I had said or had done something wrong. These acts are appropriate in their proper context, but in a time of crisis, I needed to know a God that was not difficult and simply loved me as His son. You may ask, "What are you talking about?" When you believe you have fallen from grace or when you feel a sense of guilt or shame, you simply need to know a Father's compassion, love, understanding, and empathy. You need to hear the Father's voice and His affirmation. You need to know His love. In that moment of knowing He loves you; all the difficulty becomes bearable, and more tolerable goes out of the window. It is like the two blind men in Matthew 20: 29-31 who screamed to Jesus, "Son of David, have mercy on us!" Or the woman with the issue of blood (Matthew 9:20-22). In their moment of crisis, all three merely/simply wanted to touch Jesus or be touched by Him; they needed to be reassured/ they sought affirmation of His love.

In this experience for me, I no longer wanted to follow a difficult plan to get to/reach out to God. I no longer wanted to follow the twelve steps to prayer. I no longer wanted to go through five steps before I could get into His presence. I did not want to know the Mosaic Tabernacle any longer, and journey from the outer court, into the inner court, and then into the Most Holy Place. I needed to realize that I was in God's presence at all times (and He in mine). No matter where I find myself, I am in His presence; even if I fail, realize these tests become a testimony. I needed to be reassured of my Father's presence, and not the difficulty of reaching Him. When I need Him, I can find Him. Now. The presentation of God, according to our culture, is so difficult that it is almost political and administrative. There is this climate where only the favored can get into God's presence. This notion is simply not true! We all have access to the one and only God who loves us. No matter the confusion, guilt, hurt, shame, or disappointment, the difficult God you once knew is, in fact, simple. The simplicity of His forgiveness, love, and acceptance is accessible to all those who want it.

God and I can have a conversation and He can simply whisper to me with His love. I want to say to every reader: wash your mind of the difficulty of getting to God and know Him through the beauty of the ministry of Christ. Biblically, when men were hurting or needed Him, they simply went to Him and received from Him. They simply touched Him. They simply had a conversation with Him and accepted their worth in Him. In truth, Christ remains the same: today, yesterday, tomorrow, and forever.

I want to apologize for how difficult we have made God. He loves you. He accepts you. He wants to have communion and fellowship with you. I invite you into the simplicity of God's love, forgiveness, and acceptance. In Christ, you are no longer rejected, and you do not have to work to get to God. It's simple: He stands at the door knocking; just open your heart and let Him in. Accept His love, affirmation, and esteem.

There is nothing you have done or will do that can take you out of the simplicity of God. God is not difficult. How many people have been distanced from God because we have made him too far to be reached? I have found in my own experience and as I have searched the New Testament, that the Old Testament took us through the process, but the New Testament should bring us into the present understanding of God's essence. There are no steps into the presence of God. He is near. He is always present. I ask the question: Why would a God who lives in me be so difficult to reach? Christ, through the Holy Spirit, has come to take the difficulty away so that when we want to commune with the God of the heavens and the earth, he is nigh (close, near) to us— taking away all difficulty of reaching or communing with Him.

Chapter 5

Will They Forgive Me?

The mystery behind this particular chapter is based on the theological atmosphere I created where the standard of behavior should be so high and also impeccable. I created a persona that I had to do everything right: Follow the Ten Commandments, so to speak. I had to make sure that I do not commit adultery or get caught in adultery or divorce under any circumstances because those were acts of imperfection. It took me years of tears and heartache to deal with the misery and the loneliness as a human being before I could reach that tough place of being imperfect. I had been wounded by the pain of some inappropriate relationships and demeaning considerations that made me hurt even more because of emotional needs, physical needs, or simply because of sin. It took years to make a decision to divorce because I was tortured by whether my congregation would forgive me for deciding to divorce. Would my community understand? Quite frankly, some of the things I feared did come true.

I had a ministry itinerary where I was on the road traveling two or three times a month. For several years, that was reduced down to some months I did not have any preaching assignments outside of pastoral ministry. Doors did close. Preachers did find me to be a liability. It did not matter what some of them were dealing with, in terms of sin, some closed their doors to my preaching for them because of the mark of divorce on me. I was fearful and it was hurtful to me. The situation was difficult for me to leap into my decision. I was concerned about how my congregation would see me, including my sons and daughters in ministry. I also worried about how people who had loved me and walked with me and my wife for years would perceive me. Would I be looked at as the bad guy? It was said of me that the divorce had to be my fault if I left my wife. A stigma was associated with my decision, so I questioned and struggled over the agony of whether people would forgive me or understand. Can I make the decision without having to explain the full details? Can I make the decision without having to justify my actions/behavior? Can I make the decision without having to defend myself?

God told me that to defend myself always requires the possibility of exposing someone else. It was with that thought in mind that I had to live with looking like I was totally wrong, and I *was* wrong about some things. It looked as if the divorce was all my fault, and it was my fault to some degree. I lived with the perception that it was all my fault because I had no *real* reason to be divorcing my wife. No matter how many people I had walked with through marriage difficulties and given grace to others, for the first time in my life, I questioned whether divorce is a sin and if I would ever be able to remarry. I searched the scriptures to find answers, but for the first time, I had given it such deep thought that I pondered if divorce was an unpardonable sin. Prior to this, I had not given much thought to the consequences of divorce. I had not thought about those who had gone through a divorce and were now struggling with feeling like second-class citizens. Some never felt absolutely, totally, irrefutably a whole Christian following a divorce. I did not consider the pressure to re-marry so others could find me an acceptable individual again because to be divorced or single stigmatizes an individual and if the person is the one at fault, can he be forgiven? Is there grace and room at the Cross to be forgiven? As a victim, it may be easier to forgive those who hurt us, but what if the offender needs forgiveness? I need forgiveness. I admit that I am wrong. I admit that I made the decision and broke the spiritual law of divorce. Is divorce blaspheming against the Holy Spirit? The unforgivable sin? (Since when? Isn't blasphemy THE unpardonable sin?)

My study led me to Jesus. He gave us his heart on divorce. Paul did too. We have to ask ourselves, "When we are wrong and we commit the act of divorce, is it unpardonable?" Is it the sin that causes me to have to live as a single, divorced individual, or am I free to have a companion again? Based on my search, divorce is wrong, and a person should do everything in his power to bring health, healing, and wholeness to that relationship, but you are forgiven even if you make the decision to divorce. I believe you are free to receive healing and to move on. To every divorcee': there is grace, and the Cross is for you too!

Chapter 6

Will God Forgive Me?

I will never forget one night I cried profusely. I was 50 years old before I had ever lived alone. I left my parent's home at 18 and went into the Marine Corps and then was married. 30 years later, I found myself living alone. It was a very tormenting time for me because I did not realize that living alone had so many distractions. I have preached to singles; things I wish I could snatch back because being alone is unique. I know you do not have to experience everything to have some understanding or knowledge, but I was preaching in a vacuum. Preaching is one thing but having to live out the experience is a different world. I am appreciative of God's presence; of having the opportunity to know all sides of humanity.

I struggled with the thought of God's forgiveness. Divorce has such a stigma, particularly in how our culture looks at singles and divorced people. Marriage is beautiful and I believe God created it. The Apostle Paul compared marriage to Christ and his relationship with the Church; however, if we are going to look at scripture from a holistic point of view, we must remember that Christ Himself was never married. There is no evidence to suggest that Paul was married either. Jesus and Paul are two of the most apostolic figures in the New Testament, but never married yet we hinge our lives as Christians on the words of Christ and Paul. We serve a Savior (Christ) who never knew the beauty of being with the opposite sex. The Apostle Paul goes on to say that as beautiful as marriage is, he would rather believers be single like him so that the heart would not be divided. What does that tell us? We need to look at it from a God perspective and not from a cultural, conservative, or liberal perspective alone. Not every person will marry, and regardless of marriage, all people should pursue healthiness and wholeness. Those who never marry, or marry and divorce should have a wonderful life with family and friends, and learn to love *themselves.* Married people should strive for the same self-love. Neither is opposing one another. Culturally, being single or divorced is dysfunctional. If a person is married, he is functional or better than someone who is not married. This is so unbiblical. God's purpose, as I see it in scripture, is for all men to be whole and for there to be honor and respect for every human being despite their marital status. God's plan is that all people have a relationship with Him first and that our pursuit in life should be to know God and out of knowing Him, my pursuit should be His will for my life. God wants functional married people, and He wants functional singles who can be whole and responsible in *all* relationships.

What does the Word of God say about divorce? All I knew was sublimely in the back of my mind. Subconsciously, I felt I was sinning against God to divorce. Because the Word says God hates divorce and I wrestled with divorce itself and the divorce being my choice. Secondly, can I ever remarry with a clean conscious? Thirdly, will God forgive me for this choice I am making? Many nights I wrestled with His forgiveness and His love, wondering if I had made the biggest mistake of my life. How was it going to impact my relationship with my children, my family, my friends, and my community? Also, the guilt and the shame that came along with my bad choices within the confinements of marriage. Will God ever forgive me for the mishaps that influenced my decision to divorce? Of course, I was so confused and thought I would never be used of God. The struggle to work through this dilemma knowing God loves me was so real. I had a lot of guilt-driven thoughts impacting my conscience and affecting my conversation with God. I had to mindfully look at and study the Scriptures concerning divorce.

Chapter 7

When It Is Your Fault

I don't remember in my early walk with the Lord where I needed Him as deeply as I needed Him now, to walk and talk through different/difficult moments in my life. And sometimes I need Him to *silence* me through other moments. There have been so many times when I heard nothing from God. In those moments, it was revealed to me that God's silence is louder than the words of men. I labored over that revelation because of my feelings of guilt and the shame of possibly being wrong in my decision to divorce.

> **What if your attempt to fill the void of loneliness caused you to make the decision to divorce or have inappropriate relationships?**

What if your attempt to fill the void of loneliness caused you to make the decision to divorce or have inappropriate relationships? It's a different feeling of guilt and shame when there is a feeling that what happened is your fault. God revealed to me that as it relates to humanity and as it relates to His grace and love, He made provision for all men at the Cross. He provided Christ's death on the Cross as redemption because it is always man's fault. I repeat: God provided the Cross because man is always at fault. Man at his best is still a sinner, and he is in constant need of the grace and love of God. Mankind is always in need of a replacement. The replacement for man is Christ, and as man wrestles with feeling as if he cannot face God, His Father, Christ acts as an intermediary to keep man in relationship with God despite his ills, shortcomings, and imperfections. That was the purpose of the Cross. The purpose of the Cross is it/sin/man's trespasses? It's always our fault; our failures, our brokenness, our sin, our disappointments, our illusions and fantasies, and all of our bad decisions. At the end of the day, we have to ask God to,

"Create in me a clean heart and renew in me a right spirit" (Psalm 51) because it/trespasses were my fault. The psalmist, David, said to God, "I have sinned against You and You alone." Others may have been affected by our sins, but at the end of the day, it is against God that I have sinned.

We have to reconcile when we are at fault. I had a dear friend tell me recently: Own it. You have to own your decisions. I believe that is what Psalm 51 is about. It's not only a question of whether God had forgiven David. It's not only a question of whether David would ever be redeemed and be used by God. It isn't only a question of God's love or mercy towards David. It is also a question of ownership, and David took full responsibility for his actions.

Ownership is not about blaming someone else or trying to get out of a tight spot and manipulating others in the process. It is a question of whether I can own it, and if I own it, God can redeem it. If I own it, He cleanses me. If I own it, He forgives me as I have forgiven others.

This powerful revelation was needed for me as a catharsis and as a cleanser because perfection doesn't take ownership. Often what comes with perfection when it has failed is a heavy burden of guilt and shame. It is not the failure itself that causes a great degree of shame, but it is not expecting to fail that is the culprit. Perfection does not expect to fail. We do not realize we are frail as clay. And like clay, we can be molded. We need God's grace and strength operating in our lives to mold and make us into what He would have us to be. How much is our walk with God really about our own strength? When I wrap my mind around fault and failure, they should turn me to the strength of God because I know I need His grace. I don't just need His grace for forgiveness, but I need it to worship God again. I need His strength to love again. To start over. To go to people, I've hurt or offended to tell them I'm sorry.

God talked me through knowing what happened is my fault. He whispered to me, "It is always your fault." It's always the fault of humanity, and that's why I provided the Cross. Man at his best is faulty/frailty. So, I turned to Christ/Holy Spirit who lives in me, and I worship Him through the revelation of who He is, and not what I have done. I ask God to walk me through it; to grace me through it. I ask Him to love me and wrap His arms around me. With His strength and love, I can face new opportunities.

When we own our decisions, Christ takes our faults

and transforms them into favor. He takes the guilt and shame upon Himself. He was bruised for our iniquities and chastised to give us peace. A great exchange! I pray that as you take full responsibility, you will also spend time self-reflecting. Acknowledge that you made a bad decision. Own it. Talking to God and letting Him take you through the redemptive process of forgiveness. Out of self-reflection, vulnerability, and transparency, ministry is born. Then, a message of redemption is born and the partnership that we have with God becomes a vehicle to see others reborn/born anew into the Kingdom of God.

Out of self-reflection, vulnerability, and transparency, ministry is born.

Stop blaming others. Acknowledge your faults. Allow God to take away the shame and give you a new day. Even now, I see the sun rising. I see new hope. I pray the same thing for you. New hopes, new dreams, new passions, and new inspiration. I hope that you're able to come from under the tent as Abraham did and look up and out. Behold the sun/Son. See the stars.

Chapter 8

Grace-vs-Perfection

For this chapter, I want to briefly change the central focus from "Conversations with God" to "Conversations of God. What kind of conversations does God have with us? In the last chapter, I dealt with how a person handles a situation when incidents that happen is his fault, but in this chapter, I want to deal with grace replacing the need to be perfect. I started asking myself what kind of conversations God has with us. What does He say to us and what kind of conversations does the Father (God) have with the Son and the Holy Spirit about His creation? The Father gave Jesus Christ as our ransom, as our Redeemer, as our Savior, as our forgiver, and as our Healer. The Father gave Jesus Christ as *our final argument*. What would be his conversation with us if I am constantly saying to myself, "It's my fault?" What would God say to me if I always took the blame for everything that occurred in my life, whether I had a role in those things happening or not? Or if I caused harm to others, or brought shame and hurt and pain to others?

The Father's conversation with the Holy Spirit could possibly be:

> *"Go tell Victor that Grace replaces the need to be perfect; that Grace settled that need to be perfect and that he's beating himself up to such a degree that he has not accessed My presence and My grace and My love."*

Grace was given because God knew we would need grace. We are all sinners, saved by grace. We all need the grace of God, and it does not matter who we are or what our station in life is. Grace is for the self-righteous, grace is for the heathen, and grace is for the porn star just as much as it is for the virgin. Grace is for all of us! The Father is saying to the Holy Spirit, "Go tell My creation that no matter what the background and no matter what the wound, My grace is sufficient. It replaces the need to be perfect."

I would imagine that such is a conversation that the Father is having with His Son because Jesus sits at the right hand of the Father and the Holy Spirit is in the heart of man fulfilling the mission of the Father and leading and guiding us into all truth.

So, what truth has the Holy Spirit received from the Father to reveal to us:

> *"I knew you were broken. I knew you were going to fail. I knew you were not going to hit the target. I know that you are imperfect."*

I knew that grace replaced the need to be perfect, so grace is not only the starting point of walking in your purpose, but grace also tells us that we need not walk in self-righteousness nor feel like we can't ever hit the right target. Grace is for the purpose of empowering us to complete our missions on earth. Grace is for the purpose of forgiving our past and empowering our future. Wow! Grace should be constantly saying to us, "I replaced your perfection. I'm here during your imperfection. I will empower you in and through your imperfection whatever your assignment/mission/task on the earth."

Grace abounds in the love of the Father, with the acceptance of the Father and the power of the Holy Spirit. As I experience that level of love, it doesn't require my perfection, yet I want to please Him with my life. I want to please him because He gave me such extensive grace that is unexplainable, marvelous, crazy, and unlimited! I want to please Him because He didn't hold anything against me but covered me and my withered past with the power of the blood of Jesus and then graced me to live with what I've done. I can live guilt-free, shame-free, and move into my future guiltless. It's the power of grace!

I gloated in pride in an attempt to have an unscathed reputation. The Word of God says, "A good reputation is better than rubies." I am not saying that a person ought not to protect his reputation, but there is a difference in having a good name and worshipping your good reputation. (God uses imperfect people to carry out/ do His Perfect will) Some of the great writers of Scripture had horrible reputations: Paul was a killer. Moses was a killer. Peter was racist. The list goes on and on and on of all these great apostles who had frailties and issues, but the difference between many of them and us is that they knew the extensiveness and the glory and the power of grace. How can Paul, who was a murderer, go on to do such great things? He had a revelation of the grace of God, and it catapulted him into his great future with God.

God's conversation is that His grace is sufficient:

> *"Whatever argument you bring to Me, My grace is sufficient. Your imperfections, My grace is sufficient. We have too much to do. Walk in My grace. Receive my grace. Experience my grace, so we can complete your original purpose in the earth."*

I want you to hear the conversation of the Lord over your life; that the grace of God is not simply "unmerited favor," but the grace of God gives you the great honor and privilege of living without the guilt and shame of your past. And that same grace empowers you to overcome your past. That same grace empowers you for your future.

I want to share something with you about Paul's experience with God on the road to Damascus. Paul encountered Christ and Christ asked him, "Why do you kick against the pricks?" Paul's responded, "What would you have me to do?" Have you ever thought that grace was God never talking to Paul about his past? Grace is not having a conversation about yesterday. Grace is not about whom you've killed. It's not about whom you've hurt. We are held responsible for these things and God will and does hold us responsible, but we're not talking about your being held responsible. We're talking about God's grace never having a conversation about your past. He wants to have a conversation with you about your future. As Paul said to God, "What would you have me to do?" From that moment, God talked to Paul about his assignment. Those are the kinds of conversations that God has with us. God answered Paul with his assignment and his future. Isn't that the power of a glorious grace? Grace doesn't even want to talk to us about yesterday as much as He wants to talk to us about our future.

Chapter 9

The Grace Conversation

I had to eventually work my mind through the condemnation of failure and the reality of my imperfections. There is a powerful lesson of what it means to be in an intimate relationship with the Father as a New Testament believer where we have to learn the power and love of the grace of God. Grace is incredible. Grace is also an out-of-the- box experience. It is out-of-the-box because often we cannot grasp how God could love us no matter who we are or what we have done. As humans, we are used to being in relationships that easily discard us if something goes wrong, so we find it difficult to accept a situation where God is constantly wooing us to Himself in spite of our imperfections. God's actions seem outside of the realm of our reality.

After my inner dialogue of feeling worthless, riddled with guilt, shame, and fear that I didn't hit the mark, I wondered how this whole transition of failure was going to affect my life. Also, how to transition into having a conversation with God about my failure. I got a revelation about/through Apostle Paul. Before Paul was an Apostle, he was named Saul and he was a murderer of Christians. As a Jew, (Saul) was an expert on Jewish law and culture. He was anti-Christian and did not understand that God was doing something new. While Stephen was being stoned, Paul stood idly by and watched passively. I would imagine Paul might have felt a sense of vindication over what was happening to Stephen, and he felt he was right in his killing of Christians. Saul doesn't know he's about to see the light: he is going to have a life-changing, transformative moment. It was a moment with a God that he never knew. He knew the law of God/Judah/ Mosaic Law, but he discovered he didn't really know God. He knew the performance of God. He knew the perfection of God, but he had never experienced the grace of God. It is possible to be "perfect" according to the law and know the God of the law, but not know the God of grace, mercy, and love. When Saul encountered Christ (God in the flesh) on his way to Damascus, he discovered a part of God he had not known through the teaching of the Old Testament. This man had a venerable/respectable life, but the first question Christ asked him was, "Why do you kick against the pricks?" Saul falls to the ground and his life is instantly changed. He even changed his name to Paul.

God asked Saul a very interesting question. I never thought about it until I had my own encounters with shame, failure, guilt, and my past. God asked Saul only one question: why are you resisting? He didn't ask Saul why he stood by while Stephen was being stoned. He didn't ask him why he murdered Christians. Or why he had committed such offenses. I don't wonder why God didn't ask Saul questions about what he had done in the past because I know this is what humans do. Humans are always trying to conjure up past mistakes, but not God. I believe it is God's non-response to Saul's past actions that caused Saul to say to God, "What would you have me to do?" It is a powerful revelation and I believe the Lord started showing me that it was God's grace in that moment of encounter that prompted Saul to yield to God. There is no record in the Scriptures to suggest that God reminded Saul of all the things he had done wrong. Saul became a new creature/creation in Christ and became Paul.

The Holy Spirit asked me, "Why is it that you have conversations in your mind about your past? Why is it that you're condemning yourself? Why do you perceive yourself as nothing but evil?" When I don't have conversations about my past, I have conversations about my future, and God through the power of the Holy Spirit, introduced me to the conversation/conversion/salvation? of Grace. The Grace conversation ends the condemnation conversation. Grace doesn't excuse your past, but it washes your past in the power of the blood of Jesus Christ. Grace did not take away the criticism of others about Saul's past. It didn't cause others to forget who he was and his past, but it gave Saul who became Paul a new opportunity to know God through the power of the Holy Spirit in a unique and profound way. Hallelujah! Remember, Paul was a Jew who studied the law of the Old Testament. He thought he knew the love of God, but he was given a second chance to Grace. He was given a second chance to know the God of salvation, truth, righteousness, love, forgiveness, redemption, and grace. The same God who Paul encountered and showed him the "new" covenant. He wants to do the same for you!

What am I saying to you? Are you drowning in guilt and shame and forgiveness of self? Is there something blocking you from receiving God's grace? Do you wrestle with guilt and shame to such a degree that it's difficult to receive God's loving-kindness? Is it difficult to have a conversation about your future? These are the kinds of conversations that God wants to have with you. He doesn't want to talk about what you did. He wants to talk about the great things you will do. Jeremiah 29:11 says, "I have plans to give you a hope and a future." God has a future for you, and it's a good one. Look at Saul's future in God. His name became Paul, and he went on to become of the greatest apostles to ever live. God used Paul to travel, spreading the Gospel of the Kingdom of God. God's conversations with us are not about how wrong we were. It's about how right we are going to be.

There will be people who will remember your past.

Some will even condemn you and never receive your message because of the stigma/deeds of your past, but God's conversation with you is about your future. It's about your destiny. It's about His forgiveness and His grace. He works through the brokenness of our past to perfect/mend/ mold our lives for destiny. Grace is the conversation God wants to have with us, so I admonished you: Receive God's grace.

Later in Paul's journey, he asked God to remove a thorn from his flesh. Paul prayed three times and God did not remove it, but God did assure Paul that His grace is sufficient. (Even Paul never reached PERFECTION) Perhaps you are arguing in your mind about something you've done, or you can't seem to get beyond your struggles. Drown yourself in God's grace. The sufficiency of his grace is to heal us, love us, forgive us, and empower us to perform at levels that are absolutely mind-blowing, even to us.

If you are struggling to forgive yourself, embrace God's grace. God wants to converse with you about your future. If you can't get past your past, let God lead you into your future. God's future is overflowing with grace.

Chapter 10

The Perfect Partnership

It's funny that God partners with imperfect people. He partners with those who are broken, and He partners with those who have surrendered their strengths and weaknesses to Him.

The Apostle Paul says in Galatians 6:1, "Those who are spiritual restore…considering yourself unless you fall into the same temptation." It takes spiritual people who know the propensities of humanity, even as believers, to understand that spirituality is not synonymous with perfection. Paul is admonishing us to always be self-aware of our own propensities, our own humanity, and our own failures. When we are aware of our humanity, we should be more inclined to have an honest conversation with God; it's the kind of conversation God wants to have with us.

God has this conversation with us with a constant reminder of how to deal with other people – to be self-aware and that He partners sufficiently with great power and great grace. God partners with those who are aware of themselves and who are aware of their propensities and failures. Had I not experienced the grace of God, would I have been given over to my propensities? Philippians 4:7 says, "I can do all things through Christ who strengthens me." This scripture demonstrates a perfect partnership at work! God partners with the imperfect perfectly because we are totally dependent upon His sufficiency. He partners perfectly with the imperfect because it is the imperfect who realize the total sufficiency of His grace (2 Corinthians). God's grace is sufficient. The word "sufficient" is so powerful. It is derived from the Greek word (Hi CRONUS), which means "to arrive." It also means: It's ample, fits, able, in perfect amount; it's enough; it's good, and it's large. The sufficiency of God's grace is ample, complete enough to

"I can do all things through Christ who strengthens me."

cause us to arrive. His grace is good enough, great enough, and large enough – to cause us to arrive.

The Apostle Paul had a thorn in his side, but he was assured of God's grace. The conversation that the Father had with him was about the competency of the grace of God. God's grace is enough!

God's grace is large enough to sustain you, so God takes the imperfect and connects it to His perfect grace and says, "My grace is ample enough, awesome enough, and bountiful enough to sustain you, work with you, and make you usable." That's the kind of conversation God has with us. Only the imperfect can lean on God's grace and know the power of it, then give it to others. When we have experienced God's grace, we should be able to harness the fruit of the spirit to be patient with others. It is this revelation that causes us to restore those who need restoration. We are compelled to be a place of refuge and encouragement to those who need it. Even when the Apostle Paul talked about his accomplishments, he was careful not to take credit for his own works. He cited his accomplishments as dung. He realized it was God's sufficiency that sustained him. Our reputation and our popularity mean nothing if we don't have a real revelation of how competent God's grace is.

God makes us aware of our imperfections not to shame us, but to make us more aware of the competency of God's grace. It is the revelation of God's grace that causes us to give Him glory for the things He has done for us. His glory extends into His forgiveness, His love, and His mercy toward us. It is also this revelation, despite our frailties, that causes us to want to be used of God to reach others who need Him and need to experience His grace.

Chapter 11

Relax

Relax. That's what I heard the Lord say to me as I was writing this book. I knew it was the Holy Spirit speaking to me because I am a Type A personality. From the time I was a child until now and throughout various periods of my adult life, including military service, a career in government, corporate trainer, international traveler, and working with various types of agencies from government to education training and empowering people, I have lived life under pressure with a drive to perform and perform well. My drive to perform well has driven me into living life under the stress to succeed, and as a result, I have found difficulty relaxing.

Because I have endeavored to lead a very purpose-driven life and tried to mark my life at every turn, I believe God would tell me to relax. I cannot and do not have the ability to figure everything out.

Proverbs says, "Many are the plans of a man…" All of us have strategies and plans to make things come to pass in our lives. Many of us have things that we want to do – dreams and visions. When we go after those dreams and visions, we have an urgency to make things happen. We find ourselves speeding through life, but the Lord says to us, "Relax. Rest. Come to me all ye that are burdened and are heavy laden, and I will give you rest." God wants to reassure us that what He has spoken over our lives will come to pass.

It is important to know that even a purpose-driven life can have failure, obstacles, and distractions. These things can result in delays. We all have been confronted with distractions such as career changes, family situations, finances, or other life events that may cause temporary or permanent shifts in priorities. Often, we do not see distractions coming, so they may blindside us, and before we know it, a crisis has ensued, and our priorities have shifted. The interesting thing about life is that distractions and crises are not subject to our plans. We can prepare well, but life still throws a curve ball into the game plans – what an amazing shock to the psyche of any person who is a planner or thinker! That kind of person usually has everything pulled together and accomplishes what s/he sets out to do. However, it is then that life hits you, quite suddenly, with something for which you were not prepared. Your psyche, emotions, and spirit are now thrust into a whirlwind because something happened that wasn't planned. If you're not careful, several things can happen at once.

First, you will live your lives as if God doesn't exist. You will live your lives as if every race you run, or every accomplishment has been achieved alone – without God and without the help and support of others. This attitude or thinking is known as the glory of me, and it isn't a partnership with God. With that in mind, I understand now why God told me to relax; it's because He is Sovereign. God knows how to take those unplanned things in our lives and work them all for our good (Romans 8:28). We can relax because God says, "I got you!" Even if we make wrong decisions or intentionally do something out of the will of God, we can repent and relax in God because we know we have the assurance of God's love, and His promises are always true. God knows we have plans, and He is not opposed to all our plans. In fact, some of our plans, God put in our hearts, but God wants to settle in us the need to work alone. There are times when God wants us to abandon our plans and surrender to His will, His plans for our lives. Then when things do not go the way, we want them to go, and we fail, we know God is working on our behalf. God knows exactly how to handle our failures. He will tell us to relax, and we'll panic, wondering how God could tell us to relax when life all around us is falling apart. Sometimes we need to fail, so we are reminded that God gives, and The Lord takes, BLESSED IS THE NAME OF THE LORD.

Secondly, according to Psalm 37:23, "The steps of a good man are ordered by the Lord." You are a good man or a good woman. God has all your steps, so relax. Even the steps that are your mistakes and failures are in the plan of God. I want you to consider this: Couldn't God have been in some of the mistakes and failures, too? Yes! Why? Well, to create in us dependence upon Him. Relax.

He's got you. God loved you so much that He gave His Son for you, so you can relax. God's got all your failures, hurts, and wrong turns in His hands. Relax.

Some lasting points I want you to ponder:

1. **You are not living life alone.**

2. **God has forgiven you, and He loves you.**

3. **All things do work together for our good.**

Life is like a soup, and as the Master Chef, God takes all ingredients and makes a great soup – the soup of life. He creates a beautiful mixture of ingredients, a real mixed bag. Please take note that soup/life may not always be tasty or smell great or be beautiful. Bless the Lord anyway for having life and any of the five senses.

God takes the ashes of our lives, shovels them together and mixes them up. He also takes marred clay, according to Jeremiah 18, and makes it into a beautiful subject of His image and He uses the clay for His purpose. For everything that has happened in your life, God was aware of it all, and it is usable to Him. Knowing He is working, we can relax.

Chapter 12

Questions and Conversations

God our Father is the Great Conversationalist. I am discovering with research and mainly through my own personal journey with the Lord that God is having a lot of conversations with us. It is also present in the Scriptures that God met with men, talked with them, and gave them instructions. It is in communing with God that we find men of old bowing before Him and seeking Him for guidance.

God meets with us, and it is because of His sovereignty, His presence, and His love for us that we fall before Him in His presence, understanding that He's our Father and our Maker. The concept of conversing with God doesn't replace prayer. I want to emphasize that I'm not saying that we pray, and God talks. We pray, but God talks. I do believe that much of what we characterize as prayer is a monologue. We talk but do not allow God to respond or interact with us. What we do mostly is not dialogue. We are not in an exchange with our Creator.

I'll never forget one of my great mentors, Dr. Milton Merritt, who said to me that often God wants us to be quiet so He can talk to us, and I found this concept to be true in my personal experience. I don't want to stereotype anyone neither am I suggesting that anyone's prayer life is a monologue instead of a dialogue with God. However, I have heard hundreds of people pray publicly and privately, and I have found that many were doing a lot of talking but not many take the time to wait on God to answer. In Exodus, God fed the children of Israel manna from heaven; the Hebrew meaning of manna is God "fed them with a question." Feeding them with a question suggests to me that God wants to feed us with a question for dialogue, not simply a monologue. The Holy Spirit lives inside us, and His role is to converse with us, to talk with us in order to lead and guide us. Those terms suggest to me that God wants to have conversations with us now. In the New Testament, almost every encounter Jesus had started with a conversation. People's lives were transformed through conversations with Jesus. I think a conversation with the Holy Spirit offers a needed perspective because conversations make us more relational with God versus His simply being a distant God who is apart from us. I contend that conversation suggests deeper intimacy than sometimes prayer. When Jesus met the woman at the well (John 4), she had a conversation with Emmanuel, God with us.

Jesus invited His first few apostles into a Kingdom assignment by saying, "Come and let me make you fishers of men." These men walked with Jesus. Jesus also had a life-changing conversation with Nicodemus. We see Nicodemus coming to Jesus at night to gain understanding about being born again. Jesus explained to him the secret of the Kingdom of God. He learned about the Conversations of God. There are many examples in the Word of God where Jesus engaged in conversations with all kinds of people. Those people encountered Him, and He engaged them. For example, Zacchaeus was a man who had stolen and taken from people. Jesus had a conversation with him about how to return those goods and reap what real repentance is about. Jesus also had a conversation with Mary and Martha when he visited their home. Martha complained that Mary had left her alone to work while Mary sat and listened to Jesus. Jesus told Martha to leave Mary alone because Mary had chosen the better part. Perhaps Mary recognized that she may not have much time with Christ, so she did not want to miss any time with Him. Then there's Moses who twice, over the course of his ministry, spent 40 days talking with God. Saul became Paul on the road to Damascus; he encountered Jesus, and it changed his life. Afterwards, Paul went to the desert of Arabia and spent three and a half years with Christ. Prayer is inclusive of a conversation with God – dialogue, not monologue. Sometimes it includes waiting to listen.

As you move forward, consider these points:

1. **Listen. Ask God questions. Wait for an answer. Let God ask you a few questions.**

2. **Don't talk so much. Sometimes dialogue means listening to your spirit.**

3. **God wants your spirit to merge with His Spirit. What a powerful concept!**

God really wants to talk with us. Prayer is really about conversations with God.

Chapter 13

You Can't Forgive Yourself

Psalm 86:5 says, "You are forgiving and good oh Lord, abounding in love to all who call on You." It's a phenomenal revelation and an awakening of a biblical truth. It's interesting when there's a deep need for biblical truth or revelation that we then run back to the word of the Lord. I was in my pastoral clinical training (CPE) for clinically trained chaplains. Typically, most chaplains take three to five CPE units – CPE 1, CPE 2, and within that formal training, a CPE training that requires new dimensions each time someone takes the course. A chaplain may take four units of CPE training, but all of them are different dimensions within that clinical unit.

I remember my most recent chaplaincy mentor, Dr. Lewis. When I began work on the CPE, I was at a transitional moment in my life. The Holy Spirit was dealing with my heart, and I was entering a new season in my life. I was coming out of a difficult season, but at the same time, there was this new budding taking place in my life. I was receiving a new understanding of God's grace and His forgiveness. One day in class, Dr. Lewis said, "Part of your problem, Victor, is you're not biblical in your forgiveness." He went on to say that the Bible never talks about forgiveness of self. He mentioned that a person can't forgive himself, and that notion is more of a humanistic, psychological interjection into scripture that sounds biblical but has no biblical basis. So, he supposed that the very concept might be warfare about forgiveness: getting past what you did, getting past what may have happened, getting past what decisions you made that led to regret, and the warfare to forgive yourself. He then went on to say that biblical practice with an understanding of God's grace and God's Spirit brings biblical reward. I repeat: Biblical practice with understanding God's grace and God's Spirit brings biblical reward. So, if you practice biblical truths, you might get a biblical outcome.

Dr. Lewis reiterated that the Bible talks about God forgiving us, not our forgiving ourselves. I began to realize that we humans have put so much on ourselves. In essence, this is what having a conversation with God and allowing Him to talk us through our issues is all about. I realized in my own life that I was subject to performing and measuring up to God's standards. This need to perform is why I had such a difficult time getting past my decision to divorce or getting past some sin or weakness I felt I had succumbed to. I found it difficult to get past anything that made me feel like I was not measuring up. It was almost as if I related to God from a grade perspective. You know. You get an A in class if you pass all the tests; you get a B if you get a few wrong answers; and you get a C if you get more answers wrong. We've put so much on ourselves, and we've put nothing on the Cross. We put so much on our performance and pleasing God, and we do not allow the Cross to work in our lives. We leave no room for the blood of Jesus or the grace of God to work in us. We reversed the working of the Holy Spirit.

I found myself like Saul before he became Paul. I bragged that I lived according to the word of God. What was

Paul's brag? He bragged that he was a Pharisee of the Pharisees. He said he was a Jew, circumcised on the eighth day, according to the law. Paul said, "I was blameless." That was almost my approach to God as well as a New Testament believer. Yes, it's important that we please God. Yes, it's important that we attempt to rely upon the power of the Holy Spirit to live His word, but IT IS NOT ABOUT US. When Dr. Lewis said I couldn't forgive myself because it is not biblical to do so, I understood that to do so would make everything about me. It would be about my ability or capacity to perform when it is the role of the Holy Spirit to invite me to accept God's forgiveness. When we accept God's forgiveness, He gives us the power to forgive others. A law of exchange takes place when you receive God's forgiveness, and you understand the power of His forgiveness toward you. You don't forgive yourself. You can't. It's about God forgiving you, and you now freely give away to others what you've received of Him.

When we accept God's forgiveness, He gives us the power to forgive others.

I hear what you're saying, "The Bible says to love my neighbor as myself, to love God with all my heart, and to love our neighbor as ourselves." It's important that we love ourselves so that we have the capacity to love our neighbor, but as it relates to the forgiveness of God, when we take away His forgiveness, it directly targets guilt and shame. Once you get a revelation of His forgiveness, it's then that you submit to His work. I abandoned my need to forgive myself and realized it is the work of God in my life. We were not designed to carry the weight of guilt or shame. Jesus bore the cross for us; He was sent to redeem our sin and shame. All of the self-hating behavior that we have was designed to be carried on the shoulders of Jesus Christ at the Cross, and when He resurrected, He settled your forgiveness freely. Now, you give forgiveness away to other people.

When I can't forgive myself; I have made it about me, but once I understand the magnitude of His forgiveness, and I'm grateful for it, it should be easier to forgive others. That's right! Opening our hearts to biblical forgiveness may give us the heart to forgive others and walk in the freedom and liberty that forgiveness provides. Stop carrying the load of guilt and shame and give the load to Jesus who has paid the debt to carry it.

About The Author

Victor L. Powell is a native of Chicago, Illinois. He left Chicago to serve on active duty in the United States Marine Corps for seven years before being honorably discharged as a Sergeant E-5. He then served two years in the U. S. Marine Corps Reserves and was honorably discharged as a Staff Sergeant E-6. Since 1990, Powell has served as the Senior Leader of Rhema Word Cathedral, in Albany, Georgia.

Powell has extensive experience in law enforcement, including years of service in the criminal justice system. Mr. Powell served as a sergeant at the Georgia Probation Detention Center and was the first trainer at Autry State Prison. He was promoted to the Corrections Academy as a

Public Safety Instructor II at the Georgia Public Safety Training Center (GPSTC) in Forsyth, Georgia. Powell was then promoted to Georgia Juvenile Justice Academy as a Public Safety Instructor III, in Forsyth, Georgia. He has provided training for law enforcement agencies and corresponding professional organizations, colleges and universities, the Housing Authority (regional, state, and local) on Team-Building, Diversity, Conflict Resolution, and Resilient Leadership. He now serves as a Subject Matter Expert for the SAFLEO (Suicide Awareness for Law Enforcement Officers) Program for the Bureau of Justice Assistance.

In honor of his hard work and diligence as a world citizen, Powell was recognized by the Georgia House of Representatives and was honored through an official Resolution by the U. S. Congress. He also received an official proclamation by the Albany mayor's office, and was the recipient of the Martin Luther King, Jr. Service Award.

Mr. Powell has authored more than five books and received an honorary doctorate in theology from Western Theological Seminary. He earned a bachelor's degree in biblical studies from Moriah Bible College and has trained for certification as a life coach. Powell is also a certified mediator. Additionally, he has completed studies in the Clinical Pastoral Chaplaincy program and was an on-staff chaplain at Tallahassee Memorial Hospital.

CONVERSATIONS
with GOD
JOURNAL

Conversation Notes: ________________________________

Conversation Notes: ______________________________

Conversation Notes: ____________________________

Conversation Notes: ______________________________

Conversation Notes: ______________________________

Conversation Notes: ______________________________

____

____

____

____

____

____

____

____

____

____

____

____

____

____

____

____

____

____

____

____

____

____

____

Conversation Notes: ______________________________

Conversation Notes: ______________________________

Conversation Notes: ________________________________

____
____
____
____
____
____
____
____
____
____
____
____
____
____
____
____
____
____
____
____
____
____
____

Conversation Notes: ____________________________

Conversation Notes: ______________________________

Conversation Notes: ______________________________

Conversation Notes: ____________________________

Conversation Notes: ______________________________

Conversation Notes: ______________________________

Conversation Notes: ______________________________

Conversation Notes: ____________________________

Conversation Notes: ______________________________

Conversation Notes: ______________________________

Conversation Notes: ____________________________

www.ingramcontent.com/pod-product-compliance
Lightning Source LLC
Chambersburg PA
CBHW070516200726
48293CB00007B/2571
9781955107808